ABU DHABI'S AI AMBITION

Steve k. Bryant

Copyright

Copyright © 2024 by Steve k. Bryant

All rights reserved. No part of this publication may be reproduced, distributed, or transmitted in any form or by any means, including photocopying, recording, or other electronic or mechanical methods, without the prior written permission of the publisher, except in the case of brief quotations embodied in critical reviews and certain other noncommercial uses permitted by copyright law.

Table of Contents

Introduction 8

Chapter 1 11

AI Ambitions in the UAE 11

    The UAE's AI Development's Historical Context 11

    Omar Al Olama's Appointment and His Function.... 13

    The objectives and benchmarks of the UAE's national AI strategy 15

    Important Initiatives and Programs 19

Chapter 2 24

Using AI to Diversify the Economy 24

    AI's Economic Importance for the UAE 24

    PwC Middle East Report: Artificial Intelligence's Possible Impact on the UAE Economy 27

    Case Studies of AI Implementation in the Logistics, Energy, and Other Industries 29

Chapter 3 38

Investments and Strategic Alliances 38

    The UAE-US AI Partnership in Brief 38

    Microsoft's G42 Investment of $1.5 Billion 41

    Consequences of Breaking Off Relations with Chinese Hardware Vendors 44

    influence on the artificial intelligence sector 46

    US Export Controls' Effects on Semiconductor Technologies and AI 47

    The Purpose of Export Regulations 47

Chapter 4 53

The Global Effects of G42 53

    Context and Organization of G42 53

    Examines and Debates Regarding G42's Chinese Relationships 57

    The Effect of Disputations on G42's Functions 60

    Realignments and Post-Investment Strategies 61

Chapter 5 66

Policy and Governance of AI in the UAE 66

Programs for Public Officials to Learn AI 66

Dubai's Prompt Engineering Initiative to Teach a Million Citizens Overview 71

Introduction to Regulatory Frameworks and Ethical Considerations for AI 75

Chapter 6 81

Projects and Innovations in Technology 81

The Evolution and Significance of Falcon10B Preface 81

Working together to develop Jais, the Generative AI Model for Arabic and English 84

Prospects for Future LLMs in Underrepresented Languages: An Overview 88

Chapter 7 93

The Battle for Global AI Domination 93

The Geopolitical Setting: China vs. the US in the AI Race 93

Introduction: The UAE's International Relations Balancing Act 97

Consequences for security and military 101

Chapter 8 104

Situational Analysis and Real-World Uses 104

Abu Dhabi Health Services Company (SEHA) Case Study 105

Dubai Health Authority (DHA) Case Study 107

Case Study: The Intelligent Surveillance System in Dubai 108

Abu Dhabi National Oil Company (ADNOC) Case Study 110

Dubai Electricity and Water Authority (DEWA) Case Study 111

Chapter 9 115

Establishing an AI Network 115

Bringing in Talent and Establishing an AI Community Overview 115

UAE's AI startups and investment trends 120

The Function of Academic and Scientific Establishments 123

Artificial Intelligence University of Mohamed bin Zayed (MBZUAI) 125

Chapter 10: 128

Prospects and Obstacles for the Future 128

Long-Term Objectives by 2031 for AI in the UAE 128

Possible Difficulties and Obstacles 132

Techniques for Maintaining AI's Growth and Innovation 135

Conclusion 141

Putting the National AI Strategy into Practice 142

Obstacles and Adjustments 143

The Strategic Significance of US Alignment 144

Taking Up Future Challenges 147

Constructing a Long-Term AI Environment 148

Encouraging Worldwide Collaborations: 149

Introduction

A Synopsis of Abu Dhabi's AI Leadership Vision

The United Arab Emirates (UAE) capital, Abu Dhabi, is putting itself at the forefront of the global artificial intelligence (AI) competition. The UAE is putting into practice a national plan centered on innovation, investment, and talent development with the clear goal of becoming a premier hub for artificial intelligence. The nation's dedication to utilizing AI's revolutionary potential is demonstrated by Omar Al Olama's nomination in 2017 as the first Minister of State for Artificial Intelligence in history. Abu Dhabi hopes to stay competitive in an increasingly digital world by using AI to improve a number of industries, such as energy, logistics, and healthcare.

The Strategic Value of AI in Increasing Economic Diversification in the UAE

The UAE, one of the biggest producers of fossil fuels worldwide, understands how important it is to diversify its economy away from the oil industry. AI is viewed as a key instrument in this change, with the potential to boost the UAE's GDP by $96 billion by 2030. The UAE hopes to stimulate creativity, increase efficiency, and open up new business prospects by incorporating AI into important industries. This tactical change is a component of a larger initiative to create a knowledge-based economy capable of long-term stability and growth.

US-UAE Symbiosis in the AI Environment

The UAE and the US have similar goals for scientific growth, which is reflected in their aspirations for artificial intelligence. Recent partnerships highlight this relationship, such Microsoft's $1.5 billion investment in the AI group G42, based in Abu Dhabi. Geopolitical concerns also play a role in this alignment, as the US wants to keep its lead in the AI race and oppose China's influence in the area. The strategic significance of this connection is demonstrated by the UAE's alignment with US technologies and policies, such as the exclusion of Chinese hardware providers. This collaboration strengthens the UAE's standing as a trustworthy friend in the international IT scene while also advancing its AI capabilities.

Chapter 1

AI Ambitions in the UAE

The UAE's AI Development's Historical Context

The United Arab Emirates (UAE) has taken a methodical and planned approach to becoming a leader in artificial intelligence (AI), which is in line with the country's larger aim of technological and economic development. This goal stems from the nation's proactive efforts to ensure sustainable development and future-proof its economy beyond its customary reliance on oil earnings.

The UAE has always embraced new technologies with a forward-thinking attitude. Early on, the nation's leaders realized that sustained economic advantage and long-term prosperity depended on technological innovation. The foundation for the incorporation of cutting-edge technologies into numerous economic **sectors was established by the UAE's Vision 2021 and the more recent Vision 2071 programs.**

The United Arab Emirates made significant investments in information and communication technology (ICT) infrastructure in the early 2010s, marking the beginning of the adoption of AI. The government created a number of free zones, like twofour54 in Abu Dhabi and Dubai Internet City, to draw in digital firms and promote an innovative atmosphere. These areas had a legal structure that promoted tech sector growth and investment, paving the way for AI research and development.

The government of the UAE recognized an opportunity to establish the country as a major player in the AI space as advances in AI and global awareness of the technology started to pick up speed. The government realized that in order to remain competitive on a global scale, it would need to become a hub for AI innovation and knowledge in addition to using AI technologies. As a result of this understanding, comprehensive policies and AI-focused institutions were established.

Omar Al Olama's Appointment and His Function

The nomination of Omar bin Sultan Al Olama as the Minister of State for Artificial Intelligence in 2017 marked a crucial turning point in the UAE's AI journey. This appointment was a part of a larger cabinet reorganization that sought to ensure the UAE's competitiveness in the digital era and modernize the country's governing methods.

Omar Al Olama, who was born in 1990, is a representation of the young, vibrant leadership style in the UAE. After earning a business administration degree from the American University of Dubai, he went on to study entrepreneurship and innovation. He possessed the knowledge and understanding required to close the gap between policy and technological advancement because of his background in both business and technology.

Al Olama has a number of important duties in her capacity as Minister of State for Artificial Intelligence, including:

Formulating policies: Creating and executing measures to support the expansion of artificial intelligence (AI) in diverse economic domains.

International Collaboration: Forming alliances with top AI countries and businesses to promote cooperation and knowledge sharing.

expertise development: establishing projects and programs to nurture homegrown AI expertise and draw in outside specialists to the United Arab Emirates.

Public Awareness: Raising public awareness of AI's advantages and possibilities in both the public and private domains will help to guarantee its broad acceptance and comprehension.

The UAE has started a number of projects to integrate AI into the economy and society under Al Olama's direction. Because of his proactive stance, the UAE has worked with global tech behemoths, invested in regional entrepreneurs, and created a legislative framework that encourages innovation while taking moral issues into account.

The objectives and benchmarks of the UAE's national AI strategy

The UAE National AI Strategy 2031 was introduced by the UAE government in October 2017, not long after Al Olama was appointed. In order to establish the UAE as a global leader in AI by 2031, this strategy lays out the country's vision for integrating AI into a number of sectors and sets lofty targets. The strategy is supported by multiple important pillars:

Infrastructure and Data: Establishing the data and infrastructural ecosystems required to enable AI research and application. This entails establishing secure cybersecurity protocols and setting up national data repositories.

Governance and Law: Creating a legal framework that encourages creativity and guarantees the development and application of AI in an ethical manner. Guidelines for data protection, accountability, and transparency are included in this.

Education and Skills Development: To create a trained workforce, specialized training programs should be developed and AI should be incorporated into the national education curriculum. Additionally, collaborations with eminent research institutes and universities are required for this.

Research and Development (R&D): Fostering AI R&D by creating research centers, funding projects, and enticing public-private sector cooperation.

Adoption and Commercialization: Encouraging the integration of AI technologies into important industries like finance, energy, transportation, and healthcare. This includes pilot initiatives and incentives for enterprises to integrate AI technology.

The National AI Strategy's objectives

The UAE National AI Strategy 2031 lays out a number of challenging objectives:

AI Talent Development: Educating more than 100,000 AI professionals and specialists to create a strong local talent pool.

Global AI Hub: Establishing the United Arab Emirates as a center for AI research and development that draws top researchers and businesses from around the world.

AI in Government Services: Including AI into every facet of government operations to boost productivity, cut expenses, and raise citizen happiness.

use of AI in Important industries: Ensuring the use of AI technology in important industries to promote economic expansion and enhance living standards.

AI Ethics and Governance: Creating a thorough framework for AI ethics and governance is necessary to guarantee the ethical and long-term advancement of AI.

Reached Milestones

Since the strategy's introduction, the UAE has accomplished a number of significant firsts:

Mohamed bin Zayed University of Artificial Intelligence (MBZUAI) was founded: 2019 saw the establishment of the first graduate-level AI university in the world by the United Arab Emirates. MBZUAI seeks to promote AI research and development internationally and provides master's and PhD programs in the field.

AI Lab and Innovation Centers: The United Arab Emirates has established a number of AI laboratories and innovation centers. One such facility is the Dubai Future Foundation's AI Lab, which is dedicated to creating AI solutions for the public and private sectors.

AI in Government Initiatives: AI has been incorporated into the operations of several government agencies. For instance, the Ministry of Health and Prevention use AI for patient care and medical diagnostics, while the Dubai Police have adopted AI-driven predictive policing.

International Partnerships: The United Arab Emirates has established strategic alliances with top AI businesses and research centers across the globe. These partnerships support the creation of cutting-edge AI technology as well as the transfer of knowledge.

AI in Education: Specialized AI training programs have been created in collaboration with leading universities and tech companies, and AI has been incorporated into the national education curriculum.

Important Initiatives and Programs

Falcon 10B: The large language model (LLM) Falcon 10B was unveiled in late 2023 by the government-backed Technology Innovation Institute in Abu Dhabi. It performed better than Google and Meta's offerings in certain criteria. This project demonstrates the UAE's dedication to creating cutting-edge AI technology.

Dubai's One Million Coders Initiative: The goal of Dubai's One Million Coders Initiative is to teach one million young Arabs AI and coding, giving them the tools they need to succeed in the digital economy. The program provides certifications and online training in a number of AI technologies and programming languages.

Dubai's Smart: The AI Lab in Dubai has started a number of AI-driven initiatives aimed at improving citizen services and standard of living. These include chatbots for customer care driven by AI, intelligent traffic control systems, and infrastructure maintenance that is scheduled in advance.

AI Ethics Advisory Board: To address moral issues surrounding the application of AI, the Smart Dubai AI Ethics Advisory Board was founded. The board's main objectives are to detect and reduce biases in AI systems, protect user privacy, and uphold responsibility in AI decision-making.

Prospective Courses

In the future, the UAE will keep pushing the limits of AI usage and innovation. The government is dedicated to realizing the objectives outlined in the National AI Strategy 2031 and making sure AI plays a major role in the diversification and expansion of the country's economy. Future priorities will cover the following areas:

Increasing Investment in AI R&D: The United Arab Emirates wants to see more money going toward AI research and development, especially in fields like robotics, computer vision, and natural language processing. This involves supporting AI startups, collaborating with top AI institutes, and providing money for research projects.

Improving AI Education and Training: In order to guarantee a steady supply of qualified AI specialists, the government intends to increase the scope of AI education and training initiatives. This entails incorporating AI into curricula, giving grants for AI research, and giving workers access to possibilities for ongoing education.

Expanding AI Adoption in Sectors: The United Arab Emirates will persist in advancing the integration of AI technology across several domains, primarily concentrating on healthcare, energy, transportation, and finance. This covers pilot programs, public-private alliances, and financial incentives for companies using AI.

Enhancing AI Ethics and Governance: The United Arab Emirates is dedicated to creating strong governance structures that guarantee the moral and responsible application of AI. This include setting rules for AI ethics, updating regulations, and encouraging accountability and transparency in AI systems.

Encouraging a Global AI Ecosystem: Through luring in foreign talent, encouraging partnerships, and organizing worldwide AI conferences and events, the UAE hopes to establish itself as a global hub for AI. Initiatives to market the UAE as a location for AI innovation, investment, and research are included in this.

The UAE's goals in AI are part of a larger plan to use technology to promote development and expansion of the economy in a sustainable manner. The United Arab Emirates is establishing itself as a frontrunner in the worldwide artificial intelligence scene by means of calculated investments, global alliances, and a dedication to creativity. Because of the country's all-encompassing strategy, which includes developing talent, forming policies, and taking ethical issues into account, AI is guaranteed to have a significant impact on the UAE's future and long-term prosperity.

Chapter 2

Using AI to Diversify the Economy

AI's Economic Importance for the UAE

Being a major global oil producer, the United Arab Emirates has historically built its economy around its abundant fossil fuel reserves. However, the UAE has deliberately turned its focus to economic diversification in recognition of the limited nature of these resources and the necessity for sustainable economic growth. A key component of this plan is artificial intelligence (AI), which holds the promise of revolutionizing a number of industries and lowering the country's reliance on oil earnings.

The economic importance of AI to the United Arab Emirates can be comprehended from multiple angles:

Productivity and Economic Growth: By increasing productivity in a number of industries, artificial intelligence (AI) has the potential to dramatically increase economic growth. Artificial Intelligence (AI) can result in significant cost savings and efficiency gains by automating repetitive jobs, streamlining operations, and offering sophisticated insights. For example, supply chains can be streamlined by AI-powered logistics, and production downtime can be minimized by AI-driven predictive maintenance.

Competitiveness & Innovation: The UAE wants to establish itself as a worldwide center for innovation. This goal is being driven by AI technologies, which are enabling the creation of new goods, services, and business models. The UAE can draw top talent and investment by creating an environment that supports AI research and development, further solidifying its position as leader in technological innovation.

Job Creation and Skills Development: AI has the ability to automate some professions, but it also opens up new career prospects and increases the need for qualified workers. The United Arab Emirates is allocating resources towards educational and training initiatives aimed at cultivating a labor force proficient in AI. This helps draw in top talent from abroad to the area while also guaranteeing that the local populace may profit from the AI revolution.

Diversification of Revenue Streams: AI can spur expansion in non-oil industries including banking, healthcare, tourism, and transportation. AI applications, for instance, can boost risk management and customer service in the banking industry while also improving patient outcomes and operational efficiency in the healthcare industry. Through economic diversification, the UAE may lessen its reliance on changes in the price of oil and guarantee more stable economic growth.

Sustainable Development: The UAE's sustainability objectives can be greatly aided by AI. AI technology can contribute to the development of a more resilient and sustainable economy by improving waste management, boosting smart city efforts, and optimizing energy use. The UAE's investments in smart grid technologies and AI-powered renewable energy projects demonstrate its commitment to environmental sustainability.

PwC Middle East Report: Artificial Intelligence's Possible Impact on the UAE Economy

The possible economic effects of AI on the United Arab Emirates are thoroughly examined in the PwC Middle East research. The analysis estimates that by 2030, artificial intelligence (AI) might boost the UAE economy by up to $96 billion, or almost 14% of GDP. This prediction emphasizes how AI has the ability to change the world and how important it is to the country's agenda for economic diversification.

Among the PwC report's main conclusions are:

Sectoral Impact: The research emphasizes that industries including healthcare, banking, and transportation stand to gain the most from artificial intelligence. AI in healthcare can enhance patient care, tailor treatment regimens, and increase diagnostic accuracy. AI in transportation can facilitate autonomous vehicles, improve traffic management, and lower accident rates. AI in banking can improve client experiences, expedite compliance, and strengthen fraud detection.

Productivity Gains: Automation and analytics powered by AI have the potential to significantly increase productivity in a variety of industries. Businesses may work more effectively and make data-driven decisions thanks to artificial intelligence (AI), which automates repetitive processes and provides insights through sophisticated analytics. Cost reductions, higher output, and increased productivity all may result from this.

Job Creation and Workforce Transformation: Although AI is predicted to eliminate some occupations, it will also generate new positions requiring highly technical abilities. In order to provide the workforce with the skills it needs to prosper in an AI-driven economy, the research highlights the need of funding education and training initiatives. This entails giving current employees lifetime learning opportunities and upskilling them.

Investment in AI Technologies: One of the main factors in achieving the economic benefits of AI is the UAE's proactive approach to AI investment. To create an atmosphere that encourages AI innovation, public-private partnerships, government initiatives, and research and development funding are crucial. The research emphasizes how important it is to keep funding talent development, data ecosystems, and AI infrastructure.

Ethics and Regulation: The PwC research also discusses the moral and legal issues surrounding artificial intelligence. To foster responsible AI adoption and foster confidence, AI systems must provide data privacy, transparency, and accountability. Regarding these issues, the UAE's dedication to creating a strong regulatory framework for AI is viewed as a move in the right direction.

Case Studies of AI Implementation in the Logistics, Energy, and Other Industries

AI technologies have been successfully used in many different areas thanks to the UAE's AI plan. These case studies highlight the real-world advantages of artificial intelligence as well as how it might promote economic diversification.

Sector of Energy

AI-Driven Predictive Maintenance: AI is being applied in the energy sector to optimize maintenance procedures and lower operating expenses. To monitor equipment health and anticipate probable problems, ADNOC, the state-owned oil firm of the United Arab Emirates, has integrated AI-driven predictive maintenance technologies. Through the use of machine learning algorithms and sensor data analysis, ADNOC is able to predict maintenance needs ahead of time and save expensive downtime. By being proactive, this strategy increases operational effectiveness and prolongs the life of vital equipment.

Smart Grids and Renewable Energy: Artificial Intelligence is a key component in optimizing energy production and consumption, and the UAE is aggressively investing in renewable energy projects. Artificial intelligence-driven smart grids can minimize energy waste, incorporate renewable energy sources, and balance supply and demand. One of the biggest solar projects in the world, the Mohammed bin Rashid Al

Maktoum Solar Park, for instance, employs AI to maximize energy output and raise solar panel efficiency.

Sector of Logistics

AI-Powered Supply Chain Optimization: AI technologies boost supply chain efficiency and cut costs for the logistics industry in the United Arab Emirates. Leading logistics company DP World has used AI technologies to enhance cargo handling and optimize port operations. Artificial intelligence systems evaluate information from multiple sources, including weather forecasts and shipping timetables, to maximize cargo flow and vessel berthing. Faster turnaround times and lower operating costs are the results of this.

Autonomous Delivery Systems: In an effort to improve logistics effectiveness, the UAE is investigating autonomous delivery systems. For last-mile deliveries, Dubai's Roads and Transport Authority (RTA) has teamed up with top tech firms to develop autonomous drones. These drones provide prompt and economical delivery of commodities by using artificial intelligence (AI) to navigate intricate urban landscapes.

Healthcare Industry

AI-Enhanced Diagnostics and Treatment: To increase diagnostic precision and customize treatment regimens, the UAE's healthcare industry is utilizing AI. For example, the Ministry of Health and Prevention (MoHAP) has deployed AI-driven radiology technologies that have a high degree of accuracy in identifying abnormalities in medical pictures. By helping radiologists diagnose diseases like cancer and cardiovascular disorders, these AI systems improve patient outcomes and enable earlier identification.

Telemedicine and Virtual Health Assistants: AI-driven telemedicine platforms and virtual health assistants are revolutionizing healthcare delivery in the United Arab Emirates. These platforms deliver remote consultations, patient triage, and individualized health advice through the use of natural language processing and machine learning. This lessens the strain on healthcare facilities while also increasing access to healthcare.

Banking Industry

Artificial Intelligence for Fraud Detection and Risk Management: AI is being utilized in the financial industry to improve fraud detection and risk management. AI algorithms are being used by banks in the United Arab Emirates to evaluate transaction data and instantly identify questionable activity. These AI algorithms can spot patterns that point to fraud and notify security personnel, assisting in limiting losses and safeguarding clients.

AI-Powered Customer Service: Financial institutions are utilizing chatbots and virtual assistants powered by artificial intelligence to enhance customer service. These AI programs may help with transactions, respond to standard questions, and offer tailored financial advise. Banks can increase customer satisfaction and response times by automating customer care.

Sector of Tourism

AI-Driven Personalized Experiences: The tourist industry in the United Arab Emirates is using AI to provide travelers with individualized experiences. In order to comprehend guest preferences and provide individualized experiences, AI algorithms examine data from a variety of sources, including social media and booking sites. Hotels, for instance, may improve the overall client experience by using AI to personalize services like dining options and room preferences.

Smart Tourism systems: The United Arab Emirates has created AI-powered systems that employ real-time data and suggestions to travelers. These platforms combine information from multiple sources, including local events and weather forecasts, to provide travelers with customized trip plans and guidance. This enhances the experience for visitors and helps to promote nearby establishments and activities.

Sector of Education

AI in Training and Education: To improve learning results and better prepare students for the future, the

UAE is incorporating AI into its educational system. Adaptive learning platforms with AI capabilities tailor curriculum to each student's requirements and development. These systems make sure that students have a customized educational experience by using data analytics to find learning gaps and offer focused solutions.

AI for Administration and Teacher Support: AI is also being utilized to help instructors and expedite administrative work. AI systems are able to evaluate data on student performance and offer insights that assist educators in creating successful lesson plans. AI-powered administrative systems also automate grading and scheduling, freeing up teachers to concentrate more on teaching and student engagement.

The substantial investments and strategic initiatives made across a range of sectors demonstrate the UAE's commitment to using AI to diversify its economy. The UAE wants to generate sustainable economic growth, spur innovation, improve productivity, and open up new job prospects by utilizing AI technologies. The PwC

Middle East research emphasizes AI's revolutionary potential by showing how it may significantly increase GDP in the United Arab Emirates and change the country's economic environment.

This chapter's case studies show how AI is being used in real-world situations in a number of important industries, including energy, logistics, healthcare, finance, tourism, and education. These instances demonstrate

how AI is boosting productivity, cutting expenses, and opening up fresh avenues for expansion. The United Arab Emirates is well-positioned to realize its aim of being a global leader in artificial intelligence and a role model for successful economic diversification as long as it keeps investing in AI research, development, and application.

Looking ahead, the UAE's emphasis on AI will be very important in determining the direction of its economy. The United Arab Emirates can guarantee that artificial intelligence (AI) has a good impact on its economy and society by promoting innovation, cultivating a proficient workforce, and tackling moral and legal issues. In order to achieve its ambitious economic targets and ensure a prosperous future, the country will need to demonstrate leadership in the adoption of AI and a strong commitment to developing a thriving AI ecosystem.

Chapter 3

Investments and Strategic Alliances

The UAE-US AI Partnership in Brief

A major change in the global technological landscape is the result of the strategic alliance in artificial intelligence (AI) between the United States and the United Arab Emirates (UAE). This alliance has significant ramifications for both countries and the larger international community since it is motivated by shared goals in advancing AI technology and preserving geopolitical stability.

Similar Goals and Vision

The US and the UAE have similar goals for using AI: to boost technical innovation, spur economic growth, and take the lead in the race for the best AI globally. AI is a crucial part of the UAE's larger plan to diversify its economy away from oil dependence and become a global leader in technology. Conversely, the US aims to preserve its technological superiority and offset the increasing sway of other international actors, especially China, in the AI industry.

A strategic alignment of interests characterizes the two countries' collaboration:

Growth and Economic Diversification: The UAE wants to employ AI to restructure its economy and open up new markets in industries including energy, banking, healthcare, and logistics. Through collaboration with the US, the UAE may quickly achieve its aims of economic diversification by gaining access to state-of-the-art technology, knowledge, and funding.

Technological Innovation: Through research and development, both nations are dedicated to promoting technological innovation. The US offers invaluable resources and expertise to support the UAE's ambitious AI objectives. The US has a well-established tech ecosystem and superior AI capabilities.

Geopolitical Stability: The alliance is part of a larger geopolitical plan to maintain a balance of power throughout the Middle East and beyond. By forming an alliance with the US, the UAE advances US strategic objectives in the region, fortifies its relationship with a major actor in international affairs, and improves its strategic position.

Important Projects and Agreements

The breadth of the UAE-US AI relationship is demonstrated by a number of significant initiatives:

Collaborations in Research and Development: To enhance AI technology, the US and the UAE have worked together on cooperative research projects. The aim of these initiatives is to develop novel solutions and applications in fields including robotics, computer vision, and natural language processing.

Investment in AI Startups: A large amount of money is being invested in technology and AI startups as part of this relationship. These investments are intended to promote the development of up-and-coming AI companies and ease the exchange of knowledge and technology between the two countries.

Programs for Education and Training: To create a workforce with the necessary skills to propel AI innovation, both nations are investing in programs for education and training. Joint research projects, academic exchanges, and specialized training for professionals in the public and private sectors are some of these programs.

Microsoft's G42 Investment of $1.5 Billion

The UAE-US AI relationship is exemplified by Microsoft's $1.5 billion investment in G42, an AI organization situated in Abu Dhabi. This historic agreement highlights the expanding cooperation in the AI space between the US and the UAE and has important ramifications for both countries.

Information about the Investment

Microsoft revealed a large investment in G42, a well-known AI company led by a member of the reigning royal family of the United Arab Emirates, in April 2023. The investment is a component of Microsoft's larger plan to increase its global footprint and fortify its position in the AI industry. Having been established in 2018, G42 has emerged as a major force in the AI sector, specializing in data centers, healthcare, and advanced analytics.

The investment consists of:

Equity Stake: Microsoft purchased a sizeable portion of G42's equity, giving the business funds to develop its operations, improve its technological offerings, and quicken its rate of growth.

Technology Integration: As part of the investment, G42's capabilities are integrated with Microsoft's cloud computing and artificial intelligence technologies through a strategic collaboration. The objective of this integration is to augment G42's technical portfolio and broaden its market penetration.

Collaborative Projects: The collaboration encompasses cooperative research and development projects aimed at promoting artificial intelligence technology and generating inventive resolutions. It is anticipated that these projects would propel technological progress and enhance the wider artificial intelligence ecosystem.

Strategic Importance

There are multiple reasons why the $1.5 billion investment in G42 holds strategic significance.

Increasing US-AI Presence: Microsoft sees the investment as a calculated step to increase its market share in the AI space and open up new avenues for expansion. Microsoft's worldwide technology portfolio is enhanced by G42's presence and expertise in the region, hence strengthening its competitive edge.

Advancing the UAE's AI Goals: The investment accelerates the UAE's AI goals by giving it access to cutting-edge technologies and skills. The UAE's ambitions to diversify its economy and establish itself as a global leader in AI are supported by G42's collaboration with Microsoft.

Geopolitical Consequences: The investment is indicative of the larger geopolitical forces at operation. Microsoft supports US strategic goals and deepens its relationship with the UAE by investing in an AI company there.

Consequences of Breaking Off Relations with Chinese Hardware Vendors

Microsoft's investment in G42 also required a major adjustment to the company's supply chain strategy, specifically with relation to its hardware vendors. G42 was specifically compelled to sever links with Chinese hardware suppliers, such as Huawei, and switch to US-based vendors. This choice will have a significant impact on G42 as well as the larger AI sector.

Economic and Geopolitical Context

The decision to sever relations with hardware suppliers in China is directly related to the geopolitical concerns that still exist between the US and China. A number of policies have been put in place by the US government to restrict China's access to cutting-edge technologies, especially in the semiconductor and artificial intelligence (AI) industries. These actions are a response to worries about intellectual property theft, national security, and the possible strategic application of Chinese technology.

Consequences for G42

The choice to cut connections with Chinese hardware suppliers has a number of ramifications for G42.

interruptions to the Supply Chain: Breaking off relationships with reputable Chinese suppliers may result in higher expenses and supply chain interruptions. The lack of Chinese hardware vendors like Huawei, who have been significant competitors in the global technology market, could have an effect on G42's operations and ability to compete.

Expense Increases: G42 may incur more expenses as a result of switching to hardware vendors situated in the US. The cost structure of the business as a whole may be impacted by US suppliers' generally higher pricing points as compared to Chinese competitors.

Realignment of Strategy: The change in hardware providers is a component of a larger realignment of strategy in line with US government directives. By adhering to these guidelines, G42 strengthens its standing as a trusted partner of the US and strengthens its alignment with Western technology standards.

influence on the artificial intelligence sector

The choice to break relations with Chinese hardware suppliers has an impact on the AI sector as a whole as well:

Global Supply Chain Dynamics: The widening geopolitical division in the technology sector is reflected in the shift in supply chain dynamics. Supply chain security and forming alliances with reliable partners are becoming top priorities for businesses and governments, which may cause the global technology sector to become more fragmented.

Innovation and Competition: The AI industry's innovation and competitiveness may be impacted by the ban on Chinese hardware. Since Chinese vendors have made major contributions to technology, their exclusion from the market may have an impact on the rate of innovation and the accessibility of cutting-edge gear.

Regional Dynamics: Especially in the Middle East, the decision has an effect on regional dynamics. The future of regional technology alliances may be shaped by the UAE's increasing adherence to Western technology standards, which could encourage other nations in the region to pursue like policies.

US Export Controls' Effects on Semiconductor Technologies and AI

To restrict China's access to cutting-edge technologies, the US government has put in place a number of export restrictions on semiconductor and artificial intelligence technologies. The UAE's aspirations for AI as well as the state of technology worldwide are significantly impacted by these controls.

The Purpose of Export Regulations

The export controls are intended to accomplish the following goals:

National Security: Protecting national security is the main goal, and it is accomplished by keeping potentially hostile parties from obtaining key technologies. The deployment of cutting-edge AI and semiconductor technologies by China for military or geopolitical objectives worries the US government.

Protection of Intellectual Property: Export regulations are designed to protect intellectual property and deter technological theft. The United States government aims to safeguard American inventions and intellectual property by preventing Chinese organizations from obtaining cutting-edge technologies via both legitimate and illicit channels.

Preserving Technological Edge: Another goal of the controls is to keep the US at the forefront of technology and to guarantee that it will continue to lead the world in semiconductor and artificial intelligence. The US wants to keep its competitive edge in the global technology industry by limiting access to essential technologies.

Ramifications for the United Arab Emirates

The UAE will be impacted in a number of ways by the export restrictions on AI and semiconductor technologies:

Technology Access: US export restrictions may limit the UAE's ability to obtain cutting-edge semiconductor and artificial intelligence technologies. The UAE's efforts to develop and use AI may be hampered by delays or restrictions in obtaining some technology, given its status as a US partner.

Strategic Alliances: The significance of strategic alliances with US technology companies is underscored by the export limitations. Export constraints are lessened by the UAE's cooperation with US businesses like Microsoft and G42, which gives it access to cutting-edge technologies and knowledge.

Regional Technology Dynamics: Export restrictions could have an impact on Middle Eastern and other regions' technology dynamics. In order to guarantee access to vital technologies, nations in the area may look to form new alliances and align with Western technological standards as they negotiate the rapidly evolving technological landscape.

Innovation and Development: The UAE's innovation and development may be impacted by the export prohibitions on technology. Even if the UAE is making significant investments in AI research and development, access restrictions to specific technologies may slow down innovation and the creation of cutting-edge AI solutions.

The State of Technology Worldwide

Additionally, the export restrictions have wider effects on the state of technology worldwide:

Technology Market Fragmentation: As different nations and regions align themselves with different partners and technology standards, export constraints play a part in the global technology market's fragmentation. This fragmentation may affect the availability of cutting-edge technologies and cause hiccups in the global supply chain.

Changes in Technology Alliances: As a result of the controls, nations and businesses are increasingly forming alliances and partnerships with reliable technology providers. The allocation of technological resources and the path of technological progress may be affected by this realignment.

Innovation and Competition: As access to cutting-edge technologies becomes increasingly limited, the constraints may have an influence on global innovation and competition. Businesses and governments might have to negotiate a more complicated technological environment while striking a balance between their strategic goals and the constraints placed on them by export regulations.

The US and UAE's strategic partnerships and investments, such as Microsoft's $1.5 billion investment in G42, mark a turning point in the development of AI worldwide. These partnerships are a reflection of both countries' shared interests in developing AI technology, fortifying geopolitical ties, and accomplishing technological and economic objectives.

The complicated dynamics at work in the technology industry are highlighted by the consequences of severing relations with Chinese hardware suppliers and the effects of US export restrictions on AI and semiconductor technologies. The UAE must overcome these obstacles in order to achieve its lofty objectives of economic diversification and technological leadership as it invests in AI and conforms to US technological standards.

Looking ahead, the UAE's strategic investments and alliances will be very important in determining how it develops in the AI industry. The UAE can realize its goal of becoming a global leader in artificial intelligence and a role model for effective economic diversification by promoting innovation, forming solid alliances, and tackling geopolitical and regulatory obstructions.

Chapter 4
The Global Effects of G42

Context and Organization of G42
Overview of G42

Group 42, or G42 for short, is a well-known technology and artificial intelligence (AI) corporation with its headquarters located in Abu Dhabi, United Arab Emirates. Since its founding in 2018, G42 has made a name for itself as a major force in the AI industry worldwide by utilizing its advantageous location in the Middle East to promote developments in a range of technological fields. The company's quick rise and expanding clout highlight how important a part it plays in the UAE's strategic drive to become a world leader in technology and artificial intelligence.

Establishment and Goals

G42 was founded with the goal of using data science and artificial intelligence to solve some of the most important problems that governments and companies are currently facing. The company's founding values center on innovation, cutting-edge technology, and utilizing AI to provide meaningful solutions across a range of industries.

Prominent members of the UAE royal family, chief among them Tahnoun bin Zayed Al Nahyan, the group's principal shareholder, were among its founding members. Tahnoun bin Zayed's participation has been crucial in determining G42's strategic course and guaranteeing that it is in line with the UAE's more extensive national goals.

Structure of Organizations

G42 functions as a holding corporation, managing a broad range of connected and subsidiary businesses with varying technological specializations. G42's organizational structure facilitates the utilization of synergies among its many units and promotes innovation in multiple sectors. The following are the main elements of G42's organizational structure:

Data Centers: The essential infrastructure for data processing, analytics, and storage is provided by G42's data centers. These facilities, which provide high-performance computing capabilities necessary for cutting-edge AI research and applications, are intended to assist the company's AI and data-driven ambitions.

Healthcare: G42 is well-known in this field and focuses on applying AI to improve patient care, diagnosis, and treatment. The company's healthcare segment works with healthcare facilities to provide AI-powered solutions that enhance patient outcomes.

Energy: To optimize operations, boost efficiency, and spur innovation in the energy sector, G42 leverages AI and data analytics. The company's solutions are intended to promote sustainable habits and assist the UAE's energy objectives.

Surveillance: The goal of G42's surveillance section is to create AI-driven security solutions for national and public safety. Threat detection, facial recognition, and sophisticated surveillance systems are some of these technologies.

Biotechnology: To further research and development in the life sciences, G42's biotechnology unit uses AI. Personalized medicine, drug discovery, and genomics are the areas of focus for this division.

Accomplishments and Benchmarks

G42 has accomplished a number of significant milestones since its founding that highlight its influence on the world of technology:

Strategic Alliances: G42 has forged alliances with top tech corporations and academic institutions, including joint ventures with significant US tech companies. Through these alliances, G42's technology skills are improved and its global market reach is increased.

Innovative Projects: The organization has worked on ground-breaking initiatives like creating sophisticated AI models and implementing AI solutions across multiple industries. The Falcon LLM and the Jais generative AI model launch are noteworthy accomplishments that have attracted a lot of praise and attention.

Global Presence: G42 has made inroads into foreign markets by extending its reach outside of the United Arab Emirates. The company's desire to take the lead in the worldwide AI market and its increasing influence are demonstrated by its global expansion.

Examines and Debates Regarding G42's Chinese Relationships

An Overview of Investigations

International observers and regulatory authorities have taken a keen interest in G42 due to its quick rise and strategic alliances. G42's purported ties to Chinese tech companies have been a source of concern, especially in light of the larger geopolitical backdrop and the continuous hostilities between the US and China.

Allegations and Connections to China

The following are the main concerns that have dominated the investigations into G42's relationships with Chinese entities:

Links to Chinese Military and Intelligence: There have been concerns expressed by US Congressional committees and intelligence agencies over possible connections between G42 and Chinese military or intelligence groups. These worries are a part of a larger investigation of China's participation in international technological industries, which is motivated by concerns about national security risks and espionage.

Partnerships with Chinese Companies: G42 has been under fire for its prior joint ventures with Chinese IT firms, particularly hardware suppliers like Huawei. These collaborations sparked concerns regarding G42's technological infrastructure's dependability and security as well as its consistency with US national security objectives.

The Reaction and Mitigation Strategies of G42

In reaction to these inquiries and disputes, G42 has implemented multiple measures to resolve apprehensions and minimize possible hazards:

Transparency and Public Denials: G42 has refuted in the open any improper or unlawful ties to the Chinese military or intelligence agencies. The business has made a point of highlighting its dedication to upholding international norms and rules as well as openness.

Cutting Connections with Chinese Suppliers: In reaction to the investigation, G42 decided to cut connections with Chinese hardware providers, such as Huawei. The necessity to adhere to US technological standards and meet geopolitical and regulatory demands was the driving force behind this choice.

improved Security Measures: In response to worries about data integrity and technology, G42 has put in place improved security measures. To guarantee the dependability and security of its systems, these precautions include implementing strict security procedures and collaborating with reputable technological partners.

The Effect of Disputations on G42's Functions

The problems regarding G42's ties to China have affected the business's operations and strategic posture in a number of ways:

Challenges with Regulation and Compliance: G42's attempts to resolve issues with regulations and compliance have resulted in more oversight and attention. To preserve its brand and business ties, the organization needs to manage complicated regulatory settings and make sure that international standards are being followed.

Effect on Investments and relationships: G42's investment prospects and relationships have been impacted by the controversy. Because of its ties and geopolitical ramifications, some possible investors and partners could be hesitant to work with G42.

Reputation and Trust: Within the international technological community, G42's reputation and trust have been impacted by the issues. The business needs to put in more effort to regain people's trust and show that it is dedicated to moral behavior and global standards.

Strategic Choices and Transitions Following Microsoft Investment

Realignments and Post-Investment Strategies

After Microsoft invested $1.5 billion in G42, the firm changed course and took a number of strategic decisions to meet the demands of its new partner and take into account the larger geopolitical environment. These choices demonstrate G42's dedication to using the money to improve its skills and increase its influence in the global AI market.

Important Strategic Choices

Realignment of Supply Chains: G42 was obligated to sever relationships with Chinese hardware suppliers and restructure its supply chains as part of the investment agreement. In order to support G42's operations, this change has required switching to US-based vendors as well as implementing new infrastructure and technology.

Emphasis on US Technology Standards: G42 has made a commitment to coordinating its operations and technology with US laws and standards. Adopting cutting-edge US technologies, upholding cybersecurity procedures, and guaranteeing adherence to global standards and best practices are all part of this approach.

Extension of AI Capabilities: G42 has been able to quicken its R&D activities and extend its AI capabilities thanks to the financing. The organization has concentrated on creating fresh AI models, expanding its range of technologies, and promoting innovation in a number of industries.

Effect on Worldwide Influence

The post-Microsoft investment strategic choices and alterations have affected G42's worldwide sway in multiple ways:

Improved technology Capabilities: G42's technology capabilities have been greatly improved by its cooperation with Microsoft. The amalgamation of Microsoft's cloud and AI technologies has fortified G42's standing in the worldwide AI arena and amplified its capacity to proffer inventive resolutions.

Enhanced Market Presence: The investment has helped G42 enter new markets and industries and has strengthened its market position. The corporation is now a more significant player in the global technological environment because to its improved capabilities and strategic realignments.

Enhanced US Alliances: G42's links with US technology companies and the government have been reinforced by its alignment with US technology standards and its breakup with Chinese suppliers.

Possibilities and Difficulties

Although G42 has benefited from the strategic changes and choices, there have also been difficulties:

Handling Geopolitical conflicts: G42 has to handle the continuous regulatory issues and geopolitical conflicts that are related to its investments and alliances. The business needs to strike a compromise between its strategic goals and the intricate dynamics of international technology politics.

Building and Preserving Trust: G42 must restore trust and preserve goodwill with international partners and stakeholders. In order to move past previous scandals and improve its standing, the organization needs to show that it is committed to moral behavior and open communication.

Driving Innovation and Growth: G42's capacity to propel innovation and expansion in the AI industry will be a determining factor in its success. The business needs to keep spending money on R&D, look for new prospects, andstay ahead of technological advancements to achieve its ambitious goals.

The development of G42 into a preeminent AI and technology conglomerate from its beginnings underscores the company's enormous influence on the state of technology worldwide. The company's trajectory and influence have been defined by its strategic decisions, which have included responding to probes and controversies and aligning with US technological standards.

G42 will continue to be focused on improving AI and fostering innovation as it grows its capabilities and negotiates the challenges of the global technology market. The company's future and the wider objectives of the UAE's AI ambitions will be greatly influenced by its alliances, investments, and strategic choices.

In the future, G42's capacity to strike a balance between geopolitical dynamics, technological innovation, and regulatory compliance will determine how successful it is. G42 may bolster its standing as a prominent player in the AI and technology industry worldwide by tackling obstacles, capitalizing on favorable circumstances, and upholding its dedication to quality.

Chapter 5

Policy and Governance of AI in the UAE

Programs for Public Officials to Learn AI
Overview

It is impossible to overestimate the influence that public authorities have in developing and carrying out policies in the quickly developing field of artificial intelligence (AI). Acknowledging this, the UAE has made a major effort to provide its government employees with the abilities and information required to properly utilize AI. This proactive strategy seeks to guarantee that AI policies are informed and in line with the nation's strategic objectives for economic diversification and technological growth.

Overview of AI Training Programs

A number of projects to incorporate AI into its governance framework have been spearheaded by the UAE. The AI training program for public officials is a fundamental initiative aimed at improving their comprehension and utilization of AI technologies. These initiatives are essential to the UAE's larger plan to develop a workforce of government employees that are technologically savvy and digitally literate.

Goals and Objectives

These AI training programs' main objective is to provide public officials with a strong foundation in AI understanding. Through this action, the UAE hopes to accomplish multiple goals:

Informed Decision-Making: Educate officials so they may make well-informed choices regarding AI regulation, policy, and deployment.

Strategic Alignment: Make sure AI projects support innovation and economic diversification while also being in line with national objectives.

Ethical Governance: Raise awareness of the moral ramifications of artificial intelligence while making sure that laws adhere to the highest standards of accountability, transparency, and equity.

Program Organization

The following elements are commonly included in public officials' AI training programs:

Educational Modules: The educational modules address the foundational ideas of artificial intelligence, such as algorithmic decision-making, data analytics, and machine learning. The modules are made to be understandable by people with different degrees of technical proficiency.

Workshops and Seminars: Experts from the government, academia, and AI industry participate in interactive sessions. These workshops offer case studies that are pertinent to governance together with practical insights into AI applications.

Hands-on Training: Using real-world exercises and simulations, officials can work with AI tools and technologies, gaining a greater comprehension of their capabilities and their uses.

Application and Effect

AI specialists, educational institutions, and government organizations work together to implement these training programs. The enhanced capacity of public servants to create and carry out AI policies efficiently is indicative of the programs' influence.

Enhanced Policy Design: Government representatives that possess a strong grasp of AI are better suited to create policies that use AI to spur innovation in the public sector.

Better Implementation: As a result of training officials to better navigate the intricacies of AI technologies, projects and initiatives including AI are implemented more successfully.

Ethical Oversight: Well-informed authorities are in a better position to handle moral dilemmas and guarantee that AI applications are applied in an ethical and open manner.

Case Study: The AI Office of the UAE Government's Training Program

The AI training initiative run by the UAE Government's AI Office is a noteworthy illustration of the UAE's dedication to AI education. This program has been commended for its all-encompassing approach and has played a significant role in increasing government officials' AI literacy.

Highlights of the Program: The AI training program covers issues including AI ethics, data privacy, and AI-driven policy analysis through a series of online courses and in-person workshops. Renowned AI researchers and practitioners will also be giving guest talks as part of the event.

Impact Assessment: Program participants have expressed a stronger awareness of how AI may be used to public policy, as well as an increase in confidence in their abilities to work with AI technologies. The program has also contributed to the development of several AI-driven initiatives within the government.

Dubai's Prompt Engineering Initiative to Teach a Million Citizens Overview

The UAE has started an ambitious effort in Dubai to teach a million individuals the ability of timely engineering in addition to training public officials. This program is a component of a larger national effort to democratize AI knowledge and equip people with the abilities required to communicate with AI systems.

Quick Engineering: A Synopsis

Designing and creating inputs to direct AI systems in producing desired outputs is known as prompt engineering. This ability is especially important for generative AI models, like large language models (LLMs), which depend on well-structured prompts to generate pertinent and correct responses.

Objectives and Goals

The prompt engineering education program seeks to accomplish multiple objectives:

People Engagement with AI: Encourage the general people to become more engaged and literate about AI.

Dubai aims to educate prompt engineering so that common people may better understand and utilize AI.

Improved AI Interaction: Give people the tools they need to communicate with AI systems in an efficient manner so they can use AI technologies for both personal and professional needs.

Support for Innovation: Encourage innovation and creativity by giving citizens the means to investigate and test out AI-related technology.

Program Organization

A variety of instructional materials and activities are included in the program with the goal of teaching prompt engineering.

Online Courses: A selection of online courses that go over the principles of prompt engineering, including the best ways to create efficient prompts and comprehend the behavior of AI models.

Workshops and Training Sessions: Hands-on experience with prompt engineering techniques and tools through in-person workshops and training sessions conducted by AI professionals.

Community Outreach: To increase awareness of the value of timely engineering and its applications, public lectures, webinars, and community gatherings are organized.

Application and Effect

Government agencies, technological corporations, and educational institutions work together to implement the rapid engineering program. The initiative's effect can be seen in the improved ability of citizens to communicate with AI systems.

Enhanced AI Literacy: As a result of the project, inhabitants of Dubai now possess the knowledge and abilities necessary to interact with AI technologies in an efficient and effective manner.

Enhanced Public involvement: The effort has increased public interest and involvement with AI-related topics by involving a large segment of the population in AI education.

Support for AI Innovation: The initiative's skillset fosters a more technologically savvy and inventive community, which advances the UAE's larger objectives of AI-driven development and prosperity.

Case Study: AI Learning Platform in Dubai

Prompt engineering education in Dubai is mostly dependent on the AI Learning Platform. An extensive collection of instructional materials and tools for learning prompt engineering are available on this platform.

site Features: Users can debate prompt engineering strategies and exchange insights in a community forum, interactive courses, and practice activities on the site.

Impact Assessment: The platform's users have expressed increased confidence in using AI tools and an improved capacity to provide compelling prompts. Because the platform offers a place for experimentation and learning, it has also made it easier for creative AI applications to be developed.

Introduction to Regulatory Frameworks and Ethical Considerations for AI

The increasing integration of AI technology into diverse facets of society necessitates the careful evaluation of ethical issues and the establishment of regulatory frameworks to ensure responsible and equitable utilization. The UAE has created a framework to direct the moral application of AI technology because it understands how important it is to address these concerns.

Ethics in Artificial Intelligence

The following are some important domains in which AI ethics are being considered:

Accountability and Transparency

Transparency: Developing trust and accountability requires that AI systems function in a transparent manner. This entails giving people a thorough understanding of the reasoning behind AI-generated results and clearly explaining the decision-making process of AI systems.

Accountability: In order to handle potential biases, mistakes, and unforeseen effects, it is imperative to establish accountability measures for AI systems. This entails determining the accountable parties and putting procedures in place for tracking and assessing AI performance.

Data security and privacy

Data Privacy: At the core of moral AI practices are safeguarding user privacy and making sure that personal data is handled securely. This entails putting in place strong data protection protocols and abiding by privacy laws.

Data Security: Preventing unwanted access and misuse requires protecting the data that AI systems use. Putting encryption, access controls, and other security measures into practice is part of this.

Fairness and Bias

Bias Mitigation: Ensuring justice and equitable requires addressing biases in AI systems. This entails locating and eliminating biased sources in AI data sets and algorithms.

Fairness: Ensuring that AI applications do not adversely affect or disadvantage particular groups of people is a necessary step in promoting justice in AI systems.

AI Regulations in the United Arab Emirates

The United Arab Emirates has established an all-encompassing regulatory structure to tackle both the pragmatic and moral facets of AI implementation. Important elements of this framework consist of:

The National AI Plan

Overview: The National AI Strategy of the United Arab Emirates delineates the nation's objectives and focuses for the advancement of AI, encompassing ethical and regulatory aspects. The plan lays forth rules for AI governance and highlights the **Significance of using AI responsibly.**

Principal Goals: The plan seeks to encourage moral AI practices, foster innovation, and guarantee that AI technologies advance the social and economic advancement of the nation.

Guidelines for AI Ethics

Development and Implementation: To direct the creation and application of AI systems, the UAE issued AI ethics guidelines. These rules provide a foundation for moral AI activities and address issues including accountability, transparency, and justice.

Enforcement: To ensure compliance and resolve ethical concerns, regulatory agencies' oversight and industry stakeholders' engagement are necessary for the implementation of AI ethics guidelines.

Laws Protecting Data

Overview: To protect personal information and guarantee privacy in AI applications, the UAE has passed data protection legislation. These rules create rights for persons with relation to their data and specify requirements for data processing, storage, and collecting.

Compliance: Data protection regulations must be followed by organizations using AI technologies. This includes putting in place safeguards to protect user privacy and guarantee data security.

The UAE's AI Ethics Advisory Board as a Case Study

One of the most important organizations in the UAE's AI regulation system is the AI Ethics Advisory Board. The board is in charge of advising on AI-related ethical matters and making sure AI applications follow accepted ethical norms.

Board Duties: The board carries out research on newly emerging ethical challenges in AI and examines projects and activities pertaining to AI to make sure they comply with ethical standards. It also makes recommendations for enhancing ethical practices.

Impact Assessment: By addressing issues with transparency, bias, and data protection, the board's work has strengthened the ethical framework for AI in the United Arab Emirates.

In conclusion, the UAE's stance on AI governance and policy shows a dedication to the ethical and responsible development of AI. The United Arab Emirates is establishing itself as a frontrunner in the field of artificial intelligence governance with its extensive public official training programs, vast citizen education campaigns, and strong regulatory frameworks. These initiatives contribute to the larger international discussion on moral AI practices and responsible technology deployment, in addition to supporting the nation's strategic goals for technological growth.

Chapter 6

Projects and Innovations in Technology

The Evolution and Significance of Falcon10B

Preface

Technological advancements and breakthroughs are crucial in influencing the possibilities and applications in the fast developing field of artificial intelligence (AI). Falcon10B is a noteworthy accomplishment in the UAE's recent history of success in artificial intelligence. Falcon10B, created by the Technology Innovation Institute in Abu Dhabi, marks a significant advancement in large language models' (LLMs') capabilities, especially with regard to performance and efficiency.

Falcon10B development

Origins and Objectives

The Falcon10B, which debuted in late 2023, was developed as a component of the UAE's larger plan to become a global AI leader. The following main objectives guided the creation of Falcon10B:

Technological Excellence: To develop an AI model that exceeds current benchmarks set by significant international firms like Google and Meta, pushing the envelope in terms of performance and creativity.

Application Versatility: To create a model that can be used in a number of fields, such as conversational AI, machine translation, and natural language processing.

National Pride and Capability: To highlight the UAE's expanding AI capabilities and support the nation's ambition to become a preeminent center for technological innovation.

Technical Details and Novelties

The Falcon10B is distinguished by a number of noteworthy advancements and technical features:

Scale and Complexity: Falcon10B's 10 billion parameters enable it to do complicated linguistic tasks with exceptional precision and effectiveness. It can process and produce text with a depth of comprehension and nuance because of its large-scale architecture.

Training Data and Methods: A large and varied dataset encompassing a variety of languages, domains, and scenarios was used to train the model. Its performance and generalizability were improved through the use of advanced training approaches.

Performance Metrics: Falcon10B has been compared to multiple benchmarks and has shown higher performance in activities including text production, contextual analysis, and language understanding. It has done better than other top models in a number of important measures.

Effects and Uses

The effects of Falcon10B are felt in several areas:

Industry Adoption: The Falcon10B has found use in a number of sectors, including banking, healthcare, and education, for tasks including data analysis, content creation, and automated customer service.

Research and Development: By laying the groundwork for additional investigation and creativity in the fields of machine learning and natural language processing, the model has advanced the field of artificial intelligence research.

National Prestige: The UAE's standing as a pioneer in AI has been strengthened by the successful creation and implementation of Falcon10B, drawing interest and investment from across the globe.

A Study on Falcon10B in the Medical Field

The use of Falcon10B in the healthcare industry is one prominent instance. Patient management systems and sophisticated diagnostic tools have been developed using this concept. Falcon10B helps medical professionals identify and treat patients more accurately by examining medical records and research publications. This use case demonstrates the model's adaptability and potential to revolutionize a number of sectors.

Working together to develop Jais, the Generative AI Model for Arabic and English

A noteworthy technological accomplishment in the AI environment of the United Arab Emirates is the creation of the generative AI model Jais, which can process both

Arabic and English. The partnership between the Silicon Valley-based Cerebras Systems, the Mohamed bin Zayed University of Artificial Intelligence (MBZUAI) in Abu Dhabi, and Inception, a G42 subsidiary, highlights the UAE's dedication to developing AI skills and tackling linguistic diversity in AI applications.

The evolution of Jais

Context and Goals

Several goals motivated the construction of Jais:

The goal of linguistic inclusivity is to develop a generative AI model that can handle a variety of languages, especially ones that are underutilized in common AI applications.

Cross-Linguistic Capabilities: To facilitate communication and information sharing across language barriers by enabling smooth interaction and text generation in both Arabic and English.

Technological Advancement: Using state-of-the-art tools and techniques to create a model that satisfies exacting performance and accuracy requirements.

Technical Details and Novelties

Jais integrates a number of technological advancements and features:

Dual-Language Support: Using sophisticated techniques to handle the linguistic subtleties and intricacies of each language, the model is built to handle both Arabic and English.

Jais's generative capabilities are exceptional; she can produce text that is both logical and contextually appropriate, which is useful for tasks like content generation, translation, and conversational AI.

Collaborative Development: By combining knowledge from different disciplines, MBZUAI, Cerebras Systems, and Inception collaborated to improve the model's performance and capabilities.

Technical Details and Novelties

Jais integrates a number of technological advancements and features:

Dual-Language Support: Using sophisticated techniques to handle the linguistic subtleties and intricacies of each language, the model is built to handle both Arabic and English.

Jais's generative capabilities are exceptional; she can produce text that is both logical and contextually appropriate, which is useful for tasks like content generation, translation, and conversational AI.

Collaborative Development: By combining knowledge from different disciplines, MBZUAI, Cerebras Systems, and Inception collaborated to improve the model's performance and capabilities.

Case Study: Education with Jais

Jais has been used to create instructional materials and tools for students who speak Arabic and English. The model has facilitated language acquisition and increased access to high-quality education through its ability to create instructional content and interactive learning experiences.

Prospects for Future LLMs in Underrepresented Languages: An Overview

The creation of LLMs like as Falcon10B and Jais signifies a noteworthy advancement in artificial intelligence technology. Nonetheless, there is still a need to address the worldwide linguistic variety. In order to guarantee fair access and functionality, future developments in LLMs must concentrate on the many languages that are underrepresented in AI research and applications.

Opportunities and Challenges of the Present

Scarcity of Data

Problem: Insufficient digital data for large-scale AI model training prevents many underrepresented languages from being adequately trained. The lack of data makes it difficult to create LLMs that can accurately handle these languages.

Possibility: This problem can be solved by working together to provide and organize excellent datasets for underrepresented languages. Enhancing LLMs in these languages can also be aided by efforts to digitize and archive linguistic resources.

Innovations in Technology

Challenge: Innovative methods for model training and evaluation are needed to develop LLMs for underrepresented languages. It's possible that conventional approaches are insufficient to handle these languages' particular qualities.

Possibility: New developments in cross-lingual approaches, multilingual modeling, and transfer learning present encouraging paths toward enhancing LLM performance in underrepresented languages. Breakthroughs in language creation and representation can result from research in these fields.

Language and Cultural Variations

Problem: Underrepresented languages frequently have distinct linguistic and cultural characteristics that are difficult for current AI models to completely represent. Applications of AI may become less relevant and successful as a result.

Possibility: Working together with linguists and cultural representatives can guarantee that LLMs appropriately capture the subtleties of minority languages. Enhancing the inclusivity and usability of AI technology can be achieved by the integration of multiple perspectives in model development.

Prospective Courses

Increasing Language Coverage

study Priority: Including a wider range of underrepresented languages in LLMs should be the main focus of future study. This entails creating models that accommodate many linguistic communities and are capable of handling numerous languages at once.

Cooperation: Research institutes, IT firms, and linguistic associations can form alliances to promote the creation of LLMs for marginalized languages. Initiatives aimed at collaboration can encourage resource sharing and creativity.

Moral Aspects to Take into Account

Inclusivity: It is crucial to make sure that language and cultural inclusivity are taken into account when developing LLMs. This entails dealing with any prejudices and making sure that other languages and cultures are fairly represented.

Accessibility: Communities who speak underrepresented languages should be able to use LLMs with some effort. This involves offering instruments and resources that facilitate the application of AI technology in these languages.

Possibilities for Research and Education

Building Capacity: To foster innovation and increase capacity in this area, funds should be allocated to educational and training initiatives for researchers and developers working on LLMs for underrepresented languages.

Funding and Support: Projects concentrating on underrepresented languages can benefit from increased funding and support, which can hasten the development of inclusive AI systems.

The technological advancements and initiatives covered in this chapter demonstrate the UAE's dedication to tackling linguistic diversity and improving AI. The creation of Falcon10B and Jais marks important turning points in the field and exemplifies the UAE's expanding influence and skills in AI. In the future, there will be chances for research, creativity, and cooperation as LLMs will be expanded to include underrepresented languages. The UAE and the international AI community can help ensure that AI technologies have a more inclusive and fair future by tackling the issues and taking advantage of the benefits in this field.

Chapter 7

The Battle for Global AI Domination

The Geopolitical Setting: China vs. the US in the AI Race

The field of artificial intelligence (AI) is a geopolitical battlefield in addition to a frontier of technology. Future worldwide tech supremacy and international relations are being shaped by the rivalry between the US and China for AI domination. This chapter explores the strategic orientation of the United Arab Emirates, the geopolitical dynamics of the US-China AI competition, and the broader ramifications of AI for global power systems.

The AI Competition between the US and China

AI's Strategic Importance

AI is widely acknowledged as a game-changing technology having profound effects on global influence, military might, and economic prosperity. Achieving AI supremacy for the US and China involves more than just technological leadership; it also entails gaining a tactical edge across a range of industries:

Economic Impact: By boosting productivity, opening up new markets, and encouraging innovation, AI has the potential to significantly boost the economy. Utilizing AI technology effectively can result in significant financial gains and a competitive advantage in international marketplaces.

Military and Security: AI is essential to updating military capabilities and intelligence operations in the military and security domains. The three main areas where AI can affect national security are improved surveillance, cyberwarfare, and autonomous systems.

Global Influence: AI's technological supremacy translates into a global impact that sets the direction for upcoming technology advancements and shapes international norms.

US Policies and Projects

With large investments in the public and private sectors, the US has led the world in AI research and development. Important components of US strategy consist of:

Federal Investment: To ensure American leadership in the area and to speed up AI progress, the US government has made significant investments in AI research through programs like the National AI Initiative Act.

Leadership in the Private Sector: Leading tech giants like Google, Microsoft, and IBM are spearheading AI research, advancing its use in a range of applications and establishing benchmarks for the sector.

International Alliances: To promote cooperation and the exchange of best practices in AI development, the US has established strategic alliances with other tech-leading countries and organizations.

China's Strategy and Goals

China has established itself as a strong contender in the race for artificial intelligence, concentrating on using AI to accelerate both scientific development and economic expansion. Important facets of China's approach consist of:

Government Support: The "New Generation Artificial Intelligence Development Plan," which aims to make China a global leader in AI by 2030, outlines the government's ambitious ambitions for AI and makes it a core component of its national strategy.

State-Owned Enterprises: With significant state financing and resources, Chinese digital behemoths like Baidu, Alibaba, and Tencent have made significant investments in AI research and development.

Data Advantage: The development of AI models with substantial training datasets is made possible by China's sizable population and sophisticated digital infrastructure.

Trade disputes and tensions

Additionally, the AI race has heightened tensions between the US and China, which have resulted in commercial disagreements and geopolitical conflicts:

Trade Restrictions: Citing worries about intellectual property rights and national security, the US has imposed trade restrictions and export bans on Chinese technology businesses.

Intellectual Property Disputes: The two nations' tense relationship has been exacerbated by continuous disagreements over intellectual property rights and accusations of technological theft.

Strategic competition: The US and China are engaged in a larger strategic competition centered on the AI race, with both countries vying for superiority in the geopolitical and technological spheres.

Introduction: The UAE's International Relations Balancing Act

Owing to the US-China AI rivalry, the UAE, a major power in the Middle East with expanding technical aspirations, must negotiate a challenging geopolitical environment. The nation strikes a balance between pursuing its own strategic goals and allying with larger countries in its approach to international affairs and AI development.

Partnerships Strategic

The UAE has worked to forge strategic alliances with China and the US, using these connections to further its AI goals:

US Collaboration: The UAE's support of the US is demonstrated by the large investments and joint ventures made in the AI industry. The UAE's dedication to collaborating with American IT giants and leveraging their experience is demonstrated by its collaboration with Microsoft, which involves a $1.5 billion investment in G42.

Chinese Engagement: Through technological transfers and cooperative initiatives, the UAE and China have continued to have close relations. China has made investments in a number of UAE sectors, and the nation has embraced Chinese infrastructure and technology projects.

Diversification of the Economy

The UAE's larger objectives of economic diversification are strongly linked to its AI plan. The nation wants to become a global center of technology and lessen its reliance on oil:

Goals for Economic Diversification: The United Arab Emirates (UAE) has set high standards for artificial intelligence (AI) to boost the country's economy. By 2030, estimates suggest that AI could increase GDP by $96 billion. The nation's Vision 2030 plan is in line with this economic diversification approach.

Technological Innovation: The United Arab Emirates aims to become a premier tech hub by attracting global talent and investment through its investment in state-of-the-art technology and cultivation of an AI ecosystem.

Trade and Diplomatic Relations

The United Arab Emirates' strategic posture in the global AI environment is reflected in its diplomatic and trade interactions.

Balancing Act: Maintaining a delicate balance between its alliances with the US and China and its own strategic objectives is how the UAE manages its interactions with other major nations. With this strategy, the UAE may take advantage of both countries' advantages without becoming unduly reliant on one.

Regional Influence: The United Arab Emirates (UAE) has clout in regional and international diplomacy because of its pivotal role in the Middle East. The United Arab Emirates amplifies its impact and capacity to mold regional dynamics through the cultivation of robust international connections.

AI's Place in Global Tech Domination

With ramifications for military might, geopolitical influence, and economic growth, artificial intelligence (AI) is becoming recognized as a crucial component of global tech superiority. International relations are being impacted and the global power structure is being reshaped by the fight for AI leadership.

Technological and Economic Leadership

AI is the engine of technical and economic leadership, with ramifications across multiple industries:

Economic Growth: By boosting productivity, opening up new markets, and encouraging innovation, AI has the potential to significantly boost the economy. Nations in the forefront of AI development stand to gain both economically and competitively.

Technological Innovation: With developments in robotics, machine learning, and natural language processing, artificial intelligence (AI) is at the forefront of technological innovation. AI leadership translates into broader technological leadership and influence.

Consequences for security and military

The use of AI in security and military applications is crucial to the balance of power in the world:

Military Modernization: AI is changing military capabilities in a number of ways, from sophisticated cyberwarfare and surveillance to autonomous systems. Advanced AI technology gives a nation strategic advantages in both security and defense.

Cybersecurity: Artificial intelligence (AI) has numerous applications in threat detection, prevention, and response in the field of cybersecurity. Countries possessing sophisticated artificial intelligence capabilities are more adept at safeguarding their digital infrastructure and fending off cyberattacks.

Influence of Geopolitics

International relations and geopolitical influence are impacted by the fight for leadership in AI:

International norms and technological advancement can be influenced by the creation of global standards and laws, which can be shaped by nations that are at the forefront of AI development.

Diplomatic Leverage: The ability of leading nations to influence international accords and policy gives AI leadership diplomatic leverage. Global governance, security alliances, and trade agreements may all be impacted by this leverage.

One of the key characteristics of the modern geopolitical environment is the global AI power competition, which has important ramifications for military prowess, international relations, and economic progress. Global power structures are changing as a result of the US-China struggle for AI supremacy, and the UAE's strategic orientation reflects its desire to successfully negotiate this challenging environment. AI will play a more and bigger part in global tech supremacy as it develops, affecting the dynamics of international power and reshaping the direction of technology worldwide.

Chapter 8

Situational Analysis and Real-World Uses

Use of AI Successfully in Public and Private Sectors in the United Arab Emirates

First Off

With the potential to disrupt businesses and improve public services, artificial intelligence (AI) is quickly revolutionizing a number of areas in the United Arab Emirates (UAE). Through case studies and real-world applications in the areas of healthcare, energy management, surveillance, and smart cities, this chapter examines the successful deployment of AI in the UAE's governmental and private sectors.

UAE AI: A Comprehensive Overview

Due in large part to its strategic objective of being a global leader in technology, the UAE has achieved notable progress in the use of AI. The world's first AI minister was appointed, the UAE Artificial Intelligence Strategy 2031 was established, and significant funds were invested in AI research and development. The UAE's dedication to incorporating AI into many fields is indicative of its larger objective of advancing technology and diversifying its economy.

Public Sector Initiatives

AI in Medical

One of the industries where AI is having the biggest effects is healthcare, where it is used for everything from personalized therapy to diagnostics. AI has being adopted by the UAE to enhance the provision and results of healthcare.

Abu Dhabi Health Services Company (SEHA) Case Study

The biggest healthcare provider in the UAE, SEHA, has improved patient care and operational effectiveness by implementing AI-driven solutions. Among the notable AI applications are:

Predictive Analytics: SEHA analyzes patient data and makes predictions about possible health hazards using AI algorithms. Patient outcomes are improved by early intervention and individualized treatment programs made possible by this predictive capacity.

Medical Imaging: AI-driven imaging systems are utilized to improve diagnosis precision. For instance, SEHA has included AI capabilities that help radiologists find abnormalities in MRI and X-ray scans, decreasing diagnosis errors and increasing analysis time.

Virtual Health Assistants: AI chatbots and virtual assistants are used as virtual health aides to help patients with follow-up care management, appointment scheduling, and medical information. These resources enhance patient involvement.

Dubai Health Authority (DHA) Case Study

AI has also been used by the DHA to improve healthcare in Dubai. Important projects consist of:

AI-Powered Health Records: The DHA has integrated patient data from multiple sources into an electronic health record (EHR) system powered by AI. With the help of this integrated system, medical practitioners may make better decisions and ensure continuity of treatment by having access to comprehensive patient information.

AI in Diagnostics and Treatment: AI technologies for diagnostic imaging and treatment suggestions have been made available by the DHA. These resources help medical professionals detect illnesses early and create individualized treatment regimens.

Telemedicine and Remote Monitoring: AI technologies are utilized in telemedicine and remote patient monitoring to facilitate these services. This strategy improves patients' access to healthcare services, especially for those who live in rural areas or have limited mobility.

AI for Monitoring

Another area where AI has been effectively used to improve public safety and security is surveillance.

Case Study: The Intelligent Surveillance System in Dubai

Dubai has put in place a cutting-edge surveillance network driven by AI to improve public safety and city security. Some of this system's primary features are:

Facial Recognition Technology: AI-powered facial recognition technologies are utilized to identify people and monitor their activities across the city. Law enforcement may monitor public areas and respond to security threats with the use of this technology.

Intelligent Video Analytics: To identify odd activity and possible security breaches, the surveillance network uses intelligent video analytics. Real-time video stream analysis by AI algorithms allows for the rapid detection of suspicious activity and the generation of notifications.

Integration with Emergency Services: During emergencies, first responders can access real-time data from the AI surveillance system, which also makes coordinated actions easier.

Case Study: The Smart City Initiatives in Abu Dhabi

Abu Dhabi has started a number of smart city projects that use AI to improve security and monitoring. Important projects consist of:

AI-Enhanced Traffic Management: By monitoring and controlling traffic flow, AI technologies help to lessen traffic jams and increase traffic safety. Real-time traffic analytics and intelligent traffic signals facilitate incident response and traffic pattern optimization.

Smart Public Safety Systems: AI-powered technologies are used in smart public safety systems to monitor public spaces and identify possible dangers. Advanced sensors, automatic alerting systems, and emergency response unit integration are all features of these systems.

Private Sector Application

Artificial Intelligence for Energy Management

With its reliance on fossil fuels and need for sustainable energy solutions, the UAE faces significant challenges in the domain of energy management. AI is essential to maximizing energy efficiency and facilitating the switch to renewable energy sources.

Abu Dhabi National Oil Company (ADNOC) Case Study

One of the biggest oil businesses in the world, ADNOC, has incorporated AI into its operations to improve sustainability and efficiency. Important uses consist of:

Predictive Maintenance: AI algorithms are utilized in predictive maintenance to foresee equipment breakdowns and plan maintenance tasks. This strategy prolongs the life of vital equipment, lowers operating expenses, and minimizes downtime.

Optimized Production: The production of gas and oil is made more efficient by the use of AI technologies. AI models analyze data in real time and offer insights that enhance resource management and operational efficiency.

Energy Efficiency: All of ADNOC's facilities use AI-driven systems to monitor and manage energy consumption. These technologies assist in lowering energy waste and advancing sustainability objectives.

Dubai Electricity and Water Authority (DEWA) Case Study

In order to improve energy management and assist with smart grid initiatives, DEWA has embraced AI. Important projects consist of:

Smart Grid Technology: To optimize energy distribution and boost grid dependability, DEWA has used AI-driven smart grid technology. Grid data is analyzed by AI systems to find and fix problems early.

Integration of Renewable Energy: AI is used to oversee the grid's integration of renewable energy sources. Artificial Intelligence facilitates the shift to sustainable energy by balancing the grid and projecting energy production and demand.

Artificial Intelligence in Smart Cities

Using AI and other cutting-edge technology to enhance urban living and sustainability is the idea behind smart cities. When it comes to the creation of smart cities, the UAE has led the way.

Case Study: Initiatives for a Smart Dubai

Dubai has started a number of smart city initiatives that use AI to improve city living. Important projects consist of:

Smart Parking Solutions: AI-driven parking solutions make it easier for cars to discover spots that are open promptly. Parking availability is made known by sensors and real-time data analytics, which eases traffic and enhances the parking experience.

Intelligent Waste Management: Waste collection and recycling procedures are made more efficient with the application of AI technologies. Sensor-equipped smart bins track waste levels and send out collection requests when necessary, increasing productivity and cutting expenses.

AI-Powered Public Services: AI is incorporated into a number of public services, such as chatbots for customer support, automated invoicing, and online portals for obtaining local government services. These solutions improve accessibility and simplify communications with public authorities.

Case Study: Smart City Initiatives in Abu Dhabi

Abu Dhabi has implemented a number of AI-powered smart city initiatives to enhance municipal services and infrastructure. Important initiatives include of:

AI-Driven Environmental Monitoring: AI tools are used to keep an eye on things like noise levels and air quality. Environmental sustainability is improved and policy decisions are informed by this data.

Smart Building Management: Artificial Intelligence is utilized in Smart Building Management to oversee and enhance building functions, such as HVAC, lighting, and air conditioning. These innovations improve building occupant comfort while also promoting energy efficiency.

The UAE has successfully incorporated AI into a number of industries, highlighting both the nation's dedication to innovation and the technology's revolutionary potential. Artificial Intelligence is significantly influencing the future of the United Arab Emirates, from improving surveillance and healthcare to streamlining energy management and smart city applications. This chapter's case studies demonstrate how AI is being used successfully in the public and private sectors to handle issues, enhance services, and promote advancement. These real-world implementations will serve as role models for other countries and add to the international conversation about the potential and impact of AI as the United Arab Emirates pursues its AI agenda.

Chapter 9
Establishing an AI Network

Bringing in Talent and Establishing an AI Community Overview

The United Arab Emirates's (UAE) aspiration to become a global leader in artificial intelligence (AI) depends on a strong AI ecosystem that promotes the development of AI businesses, encourages innovation, and draws in top talent. This chapter examines the UAE's tactics for creating a vibrant AI ecosystem, including how to draw in and develop talent, what kinds of investments AI businesses are getting, and how important it is for academic and research institutions to get involved.

Bringing in Talent

The foundation of every successful AI ecosystem is talent acquisition. The UAE is aware that in order to spur innovation and industry expansion, it is critical to draw in and keep top AI talent.

Policies and Initiatives of the Government

The government of the United Arab Emirates has launched a number of programs to draw in AI talent from around the globe. Important projects consist of:

Golden Visa Program: Established in 2019, this program provides qualified workers—such as researchers, entrepreneurs, and AI specialists—with the opportunity to live abroad for an extended period of time. By giving people who contribute to the UAE's knowledge economy stability and possibilities, this project hopes to draw in talent from around the world.

AI Talent Competitions and Awards: To identify and encourage AI talent, the UAE organizes a number of competitions and awards. Professionals and researchers can network at events like the AI Everything Summit and the Mohamed bin Zayed International Robotics Challenge, which feature state-of-the-art AI inventions.

Partnerships with Leading Global Tech businesses: To create AI research centers and innovation hubs, the UAE partners with top tech businesses worldwide. These collaborations give local talent the chance to collaborate on important projects and get exposure to global best practices.

Development of Local Talent

The UAE is concentrated on growing its own labor force in addition to luring in talent from abroad. Important tactics consist of:

AI Training Programs: To upskill the local workforce, the UAE government has made investments in AI training programs. Training is available in machine learning, data science, and other AI-related subjects through initiatives like the UAE AI Skills Program. The goal of these programs is to provide Emiratis the tools they need to make a positive impact in the AI industry.

Fellowships and Internships: Through internships and fellowships, the UAE offers early-career professionals and students the chance to obtain practical experience. These programs, which provide insightful exposure to practical AI applications, are frequently funded by governmental organizations, academic institutions, and commercial businesses.

Support for AI Entrepreneurs: By offering tools, money, and mentorship, the UAE encourages local business owners to launch AI-focused projects. Startups are supported by programs like the Sharjah Entrepreneurship Center and the UAE Innovation Fund.

Creating a Community for AI

Building a strong AI community is crucial to encouraging cooperation, exchanging knowledge, and stimulating creativity. The UAE has made a number of moves to develop and fortify its AI community:

Conferences and Networking Events

AI experts, researchers, and business executives come together for a variety of conferences and events held in the United Arab Emirates. Important occurrences consist of:

AI Everything Summit: The Ministry of AI in the United Arab Emirates organizes the annual AI Everything Summit, which is one of the biggest AI conferences in the area. Keynote addresses, panel discussions, and workshops covering a range of AI subjects are included, offering a forum for networking and information sharing.

Dubai AI Forum: Another important gathering that focuses on AI applications, trends, and policy developments is the Dubai AI Forum. It draws speakers and attendees from throughout the world, promoting international cooperation and collaborations.

Workshops and Meetups for AI

The development of an AI community is greatly aided by local gatherings and seminars. Practitioners can discuss difficulties, exchange experiences, and work together on projects during these get-togethers. As an illustration:

AI meeting Groups: Professionals and enthusiasts in the field can network at regular events hosted by a number of AI meeting groups in places such as Abu Dhabi and Dubai. These gatherings frequently include panel discussions, hands-on workshops on AI applications and technologies, and guest speakers.

Hackathons & Coding Challenges: These events are well-liked means of fostering creativity and interacting with the AI community. Several hackathons with an AI theme are held in the UAE, where participants employ AI technologies to solve real-world problems.

UAE's AI startups and investment trends
Trends in Investments

The UAE's AI ecosystem is mostly driven by investment in AI businesses, which promotes innovation and expansion. The world of investing has seen the emergence of several trends:

Enhanced Funding for Venture Capital

Growing investor interest in the field has resulted in an increase in venture capital funding for AI businesses in the United Arab Emirates. Among the main causes of this tendency are:

Government Support: To assist AI startups, the UAE government has started a number of initiatives, including funding and accelerator programs. For instance, the UAE Innovation Fund offers financial assistance to creative entrepreneurs in fields like technology and artificial intelligence.

Investment from the Private Sector: AI businesses are receiving more funding from venture capital firms and individual investors. Notable instances include Microsoft's $1.5 billion investment in G42, an Abu Dhabi-based AI business, and other funding rounds for AI startups based in the United Arab Emirates.

Put High-Impact Applications First

AI businesses that tackle cutting-edge technologies and high-impact applications are attracting investors' attention. Important topics of interest consist of:

AI in healthcare: Startups creating AI-powered medical devices, like health monitoring systems, diagnostic tools, and personalized treatment, are drawing a lot of capital.

Smart City Technologies: Significant financing is also going to AI startups that are developing solutions for public safety, environmental monitoring, and traffic management, among other smart city technologies.

Notable AI Startups

A number of AI firms in the United Arab Emirates are progressing significantly and becoming well-known on the international scene. Prominent instances consist of:

G42: Founded in 2018, G42 is an Abu Dhabi-based top artificial intelligence firm. The company specializes in a variety of AI applications, such as energy, smart cities, and healthcare. Microsoft's $1.5 billion purchase in G42 highlights the company's significance in the AI market.

Cerebras Systems: To create state-of-the-art AI models, the US-based AI business Cerebras Systems has teamed up with the Mohamed bin Zayed University of Artificial Intelligence in the United Arab Emirates. This relationship demonstrates the UAE's dedication to using strategic alliances to advance AI technologies.

Kokorozashi: Kokorozashi is an AI firm with a focus on machine learning and natural language processing. The company offers AI-powered solutions that are utilized in a number of sectors, such as education, healthcare, and finance.

The Function of Academic and Scientific Establishments

Educational Programs

Because it equips aspiring AI professionals with the skills and knowledge they need, education is essential to the development of a robust AI ecosystem. The UAE has made significant investments in educational programs to promote the development of AI.

Curriculum Driven by AI

AI is being included into curriculum at educational institutions in the United Arab Emirates in order to educate students for professions in the industry. Prominent endeavors consist of:

AI Courses and Degrees: Courses and degrees in artificial intelligence (AI) are offered by universities in the United Arab Emirates (UAE), including the Mohamed bin Zayed University of Artificial Intelligence

(MBZUAI). These courses address a range of AI topics, such as robotics, data science, and machine learning.

Collaborative Research Initiatives: Universities in the United Arab Emirates work on AI-related research initiatives with foreign organizations and business partners. Students get the chance to work on cutting-edge technologies and progress the field through these initiatives.

Programs for AI Literacy

The goal of AI literacy initiatives is to increase public and student awareness and comprehension of AI. Important initiatives include of:

Workshops on AI Education: To inform professionals, educators, and students about AI technology and their uses, workshops and seminars are arranged. To keep learners interested, these seminars frequently include interactive exercises and demonstrations.

Online Learning Platforms: AI-related courses and certificates are offered via online learning platforms that are supported by the UAE. For those who are interested in learning AI skills, these platforms offer flexible learning alternatives.

Institutions of Research

Research institutes are essential for expanding our understanding of AI and spurring innovation. The UAE has developed a number of institutions and research centers devoted to AI research:

Artificial Intelligence University of Mohamed bin Zayed (MBZUAI)

Leading UAE research institute MBZUAI specializes on AI teaching and research. Major features of MBZUAI consist of:

Cutting-Edge Research: MBZUAI carries out studies in computer vision, natural language processing, machine learning, and other AI fields. The university works on cutting-edge projects with industrial partners and foreign research institutes.

AI Research Labs: The institution has dedicated research facilities for particular AI technology and applications. Researchers and students can use these labs' cutting-edge resources and facilities.

Institute for Technology Innovation (TII)

Abu Dhabi-based Technology Innovation Institute is another important leader in AI research and development. Among the notable features of TII are:

Research Centers for AI: TII runs a number of centers for research on AI and related emerging technologies. These centers work on data analytics, smart technology, and AI models projects.

Industry Collaboration: To promote innovation and turn research into useful applications, TII works with startups and industry partners. This partnership promotes business expansion and aids in the commercialization of AI technologies.

A multidimensional strategy is needed to build a successful AI ecosystem in the United Arab Emirates. This strategy should support education and research projects, invest in AI businesses, and draw and nurture talent. In these areas, the UAE has advanced significantly, fostering the growth of a vibrant and creative AI community. The UAE is well-positioned to fulfill its ambition of being a global leader in artificial intelligence by carrying on with investments in talent development, entrepreneurship encouragement, and the reinforcement of research and educational institutions. The strategies and activities covered in this chapter will be essential in determining how the UAE's AI ecosystem develops in the future and propelling further advancements in the field.

Chapter 10:
Prospects and Obstacles for the Future

Long-Term Objectives by 2031 for AI in the UAE

Establishing long-term objectives is crucial for sustaining momentum and guaranteeing sustainable growth as the UAE solidifies its position as a global leader in artificial intelligence (AI). The UAE hopes to accomplish a number of challenging goals by 2031 in order to maintain its position as a leader in the AI industry. This chapter examines the long-term objectives of the UAE with regard to AI, as well as the possible roadblocks and necessary tactics to keep the area growing and innovating.

Vision 2031: Tactical Objectives

The UAE's Vision 2031, which sets high standards for the advancement and use of AI technology, serves as the roadmap for the country's AI policy. Principal goals consist of:

Leadership in Global AI

The United Arab Emirates wants to lead the world in AI research, development, and application by 2031. This vision includes a number of elements, such as:

Innovation Hubs: Creating premier research facilities and innovation hubs devoted to cutting-edge AI technologies. These hubs will make it easier for government, business, and academia to collaborate, which will lead to breakthroughs and a thriving AI ecosystem.

AI Integration: The application of AI to all economic areas, such as energy, transportation, healthcare, and banking. By using AI-driven solutions, the objective is to increase operational efficiency, enhance decision-making, and develop new value propositions.

Global Collaborations: Leveraging worldwide resources and experience through fortifying international ties and collaborations. In order to enhance its AI capabilities, the UAE aims to collaborate with the world's top AI firms and research centers.

AI-Powered Financial Diversification

AI is essential to the UAE's plan to diversify its economy and wean itself off of its reliance on oil. Long-term objectives consist of:

Economic Contribution: By 2030, AI is anticipated to have a major GDP contribution from the United Arab Emirates. The goal is to reach a contribution level of about $96 billion, or almost 14% of the GDP of the nation. The development of AI technology and their widespread use in a variety of industries will be the primary drivers of this economic impact.

Sectoral Transformation: Applying AI-driven technologies to transform important areas like energy, logistics, and healthcare. This entails raising overall service quality, cutting expenses, and increasing efficiency in various industries.

Education and Talent Development

A competent labor force is essential to the UAE's AI objectives. Principal goals consist of:

AI Education: Increasing the scope of courses and programs in AI education from elementary school to higher education. The objective is to establish a talent pipeline with the expertise required by the AI sector.

Research and Development: Encouraging a culture of research and development through grants, funding projects related to artificial intelligence, and fostering partnerships between industry players and academic institutions.

Regulatory and Ethical Frameworks

The UAE prioritizes ensuring responsible AI development and application. Long-term objectives consist of:

AI Ethics: Creating thorough moral rules and guidelines for AI systems. These rules will cover topics like algorithmic fairness, transparency, and data privacy.

Regulatory Frameworks: Strong regulatory frameworks should be established to control the advancement and application of AI technology. This entails putting in place regulations that strike a balance between innovation, morality, and the influence on society.

Possible Difficulties and Obstacles
Infrastructure and technological challenges

Security and Privacy of Data

Since AI systems rely so much on data, protecting data security and privacy is a major concern. The UAE will have to deal with issues pertaining to misuse of private data, illegal access, and data breaches. In order to preserve public confidence and safeguard user data, it will be essential to create strong data protection protocols and adhere to international standards.

Coordination and Communication

It can be difficult to integrate AI technology into current infrastructure and processes. Achieving smooth integration requires ensuring interoperability between various AI systems and older technologies. Careful planning, coordination, and infrastructure upgrade investments are needed to meet this issue.

Talent and Skill Disparity

Scarcity of Knowledgeable Experts

In spite of initiatives to draw in and nurture AI talent, the UAE may still struggle with a lack of qualified workers. The issue could be made worse by the quick speed at which technology is developing and the increasing need for AI specialists. It will take continued investment in education, training initiatives, and personnel retention tactics to close the skills gap.

Enhancing Employee Skill Sets

Another problem is upskilling the current workforce to match the demands of AI-driven sectors. Effective upskilling initiatives and chances for reskilling experts are necessities for the UAE in order to help workers adjust to changing job responsibilities and technology demands.

Issues with Ethics and Regulations

Moral Conundrums

The creation and application of AI technology present moral conundrums, such as those of accountability, justice, and bias. It is extremely difficult to make sure that AI systems are developed and applied in a way that is consistent with moral standards and societal norms. In order to properly address these concerns, the UAE will need to create and implement ethical norms.

Adherence to Regulations

AI regulatory framework development and implementation can be difficult and time-consuming. The UAE will have to strike a compromise between encouraging innovation and the requirement for regulation. One of the main challenges will be to ensure adherence to international laws and norms while fostering an atmosphere that is favorable for the development of AI.

Economic and Geopolitical Aspects

Worldwide Rivalry

Major participants in the highly competitive global AI market include the US, China, and the EU, who all make significant investments in AI research and development. The UAE will have to negotiate this cutthroat market and set itself apart with clever alliances, investments, and inventions.

Variations in the Economy

The UAE's capacity to meet its AI objectives may be impacted by economic ups and downs. Geopolitical tensions, economic downturns, and fluctuations in oil prices are a few examples of the variables that might impact investment levels and the broader economic climate. It will be crucial to create plans to reduce these risks and guarantee stability over the long run.

Techniques for Maintaining AI's Growth and Innovation

Promoting Research and Innovation

Encouragement of AI Research

Sustaining innovation requires funds, grants, and cooperation to continue supporting AI research. The United Arab Emirates ought to fund research projects that investigate cutting edge AI applications and technologies. The caliber and influence of AI research can be significantly improved by cooperation with leading global research institutes and businesses.

Motivating New Businesses and Entrepreneurs

Innovation and expansion in the AI industry will be fueled by providing resources, mentorship, and finance to AI firms and entrepreneurs. The United Arab Emirates ought to construct an ecosystem that supports new businesses, makes capital more accessible, and offers chances for partnerships with well-established enterprises.

Boosting Talent Development and Education

Increasing the Number of AI Education Initiatives

Growing AI education initiatives across the board is crucial to producing a workforce with the necessary skills. To create a talent pipeline for the AI business, the UAE should keep improving its AI curricula, providing specialized training programs, and encouraging STEM education.

Initiatives for Reskilling and Upskilling

The talent gap can be addressed by implementing initiatives for the current workforce to reskill and upskill. Giving professionals the chance to learn new skills and adjust to evolving technology needs will guarantee that the labor force stays competent and competitive.

Creating Regulatory and Ethical Frameworks

Formulating Ethical Principles

To ensure responsible development and use of AI technologies, thorough ethical guidelines must be developed. The UAE should set guidelines for algorithmic fairness, data protection, and transparency. It should also make sure that AI systems respect social norms and ethical standards.

Putting Strict Regulations in Place

Robust AI regulatory frameworks will aid in striking a balance between innovation, morality, and societal implications. The United Arab Emirates ought to endeavor to establish policies that encourage conscientious AI development while cultivating an atmosphere that is favorable to technical progress.

Strengthening International Cooperations

Creating Global Alliances

The UAE's global footprint in the AI sector will be strengthened through international partnerships and cooperation. You can gain access to international knowledge, resources, and best practices by interacting with top AI companies, academic institutions, and business actors.

Taking Part in International AI Projects

Engaging in worldwide AI projects and forums will assist the UAE in keeping abreast of new breakthroughs and trends. Opportunities for leadership in the international AI community, cooperation, and information sharing will arise from this involvement.

Handling Risks in the Economy and Geopolitics

Reducing Financial Risks

The stability and sustainability of AI investments will be enhanced by the development of techniques to reduce economic risks and uncertainties. The United Arab

Emirates ought to broaden its range of economic pursuits, enhance its ability to withstand economic oscillations, and institute risk mitigation tactics.

Handling Geopolitical Change

Strategic positioning and cooperation will be necessary to navigate the geopolitical dynamics and competition in the global AI landscape. In order to set itself apart from the competition, the UAE should prioritize and make innovative partnerships and investments that support its long-term objectives.

By 2031, the UAE wants to become a global leader in AI research, development, and application. This ambitious and revolutionary vision calls for significant changes to the country's infrastructure. Reaching these long-term objectives would necessitate dealing with possible obstacles and putting plans in place to maintain innovation and growth in the AI industry. The UAE can navigate the complexities of the AI landscape and realize its vision for a future driven by advanced AI technologies by concentrating on fostering innovation, bolstering education and talent development, creating ethical and regulatory frameworks, improving global collaborations, and addressing economic and geopolitical risks. The tactics discussed in this chapter will be essential in determining the UAE's AI future and guaranteeing its continuous competitiveness in the AI world.

Conclusion

A Synopsis of Abu Dhabi's Ascent to AI Leadership

Abu Dhabi, a city long known for its oil wealth, has made a stunning strategic turn by becoming a global leader in artificial intelligence (AI). In an effort to reestablish itself as a major participant in the global AI arena, the UAE has taken a number of deliberate and ambitious actions that have altered its technological and economic landscape during the past ten years.

Strategic Alignments and Historical Context

Like most of the UAE, Abu Dhabi was formerly largely dependent on fossil fuels. But after realizing it needed to diversify its economy and ensure its continued expansion, the Emirate set out on a bold mission to use artificial intelligence. This change was prompted by the understanding that artificial intelligence (AI), a game-changing technology, might be crucial in diversifying the economy and tackling some of the most urgent issues the area is currently facing.

An important turning point was reached in 2017 with the appointment of Omar Al Olama as the UAE's Minister of State for Artificial Intelligence. Al Olama played a strategic as well as symbolic function, demonstrating the government's will to make AI a top priority and a key component of its overall national plan. His foresight and guidance have been crucial in determining the UAE's artificial intelligence goals, propelling legislative efforts, and creating a climate that encourages AI innovation.

Putting the National AI Strategy into Practice

Launched in 2017, the UAE's National AI Strategy provided a clear road map for incorporating AI into a range of industries, including energy, logistics, healthcare, and education. Numerous significant initiatives have defined this strategy, including:

Creation of AI Research Centers: A major factor in the advancement of AI research and development has been the establishment of institutions such as the Mohamed bin Zayed University of Artificial Intelligence (MBZUAI). These institutions are drawing in international experience in addition to nurturing local talent.

Public-Private Partnerships: Working together with cutting-edge startups and IT companies has been essential to advancing AI innovation. Major digital corporations have made investments, like Microsoft's $1.5 billion in G42, which have strengthened the UAE's AI capabilities and connected it to the global tech network.

Integration of AI in Important Sectors: The UAE has advanced the use of AI in a number of sectors. AI has found revolutionary applications in fields ranging from energy management to smart city efforts, where it has improved efficiency, cut costs, and generated new revenue streams.

Obstacles and Adjustments

Abu Dhabi has made great progress, but not without difficulties along the way. Geopolitical difficulties, ethical concerns, and technological obstacles have all been obstacles to the incorporation of AI. In order to ensure that AI development is in line with both national interests and international norms, addressing these issues has required adaptable tactics and continuous efforts.

The Strategic Significance of US Alignment Dynamics of Geopolitics and Economy

Abu Dhabi made a calculated decision to align itself with the US in order to maintain its standing in the international AI arena. A number of factors have motivated the US partnership:

Technology Transfer and knowledge: By aligning with the US, access to state-of-the-art technology and knowledge has been made easier. The United Arab Emirates has successfully incorporated cutting-edge artificial intelligence (AI) technologies into its national policy through partnerships with American tech giants and academic institutions.

Profits: There have been considerable financial gains from US investments in AI companies situated in the United Arab Emirates. For instance, Microsoft's investment in G42 has encouraged innovation and technology breakthroughs in the area in addition to providing finance.

Geopolitical Stability: Standing with the US offers some geopolitical stability in an era where the global tech superiority is being challenged more and more. It presents the United Arab Emirates as a key player in the Western IT sector, with potential benefits for cross-border cooperation and market access.

Maintaining Harmony in Partnerships

Although the US alignment has proven beneficial, the UAE must strike a balance between this alliance and its larger international engagements. Sustaining the UAE's strategic position requires its ability to maintain a complex foreign policy and manage relationships with other global powers, like China. The UAE's strategy for striking a balance in these partnerships demonstrates its dedication to using AI to its full potential while managing the complexities of international relations.

The UAE's AI Future and Its Global Effect

Sustaining Innovation and Expansion

AI in the UAE is expected to continue evolving and expanding in the future. The UAE expects to reap significant benefits from its strategic investments in talent development, infrastructure, and AI research, including:

Economic Impact: By 2030, AI is expected to generate over $96 billion in GDP in the United Arab Emirates, a substantial contribution to the country's GDP. AI applications across a variety of industries will be the main driver of this economic impact, increasing productivity and opening up new opportunities.

Technological Advancements: The UAE is at the forefront of international AI research due to its concentration on creating cutting-edge AI technologies like the Falcon10B and Jais generative models. These developments are probably going to have a big impact on global applications and industries.

Global Influence: The UAE is anticipated to become more significant on the international scene as it develops its AI capabilities. Being a pioneer in AI research, development, and application will improve the nation's reputation abroad and help shape the future of AI on a global scale.

Taking Up Future Challenges

Although AI has bright futures in the United Arab Emirates, a number of issues need to be resolved to assure its continued growth and impact:

Ethical and Regulatory Issues: It will be essential to address ethical and regulatory issues as AI technology advance. In order to ensure responsible AI development, the UAE will need to create and implement frameworks that address concerns including data privacy, algorithmic fairness, and transparency.

Talent and Skills Development: Maintaining innovation will require closing the talent gap and creating a skilled labor force. To satisfy the expectations of the AI industry, the UAE needs to keep funding initiatives for education, training, and upskilling.

Geopolitical and Economic Risks: It will take strategic insight and flexibility to navigate through geopolitical tensions and economic uncertainties. Maintaining the UAE's place in the global AI landscape will depend on its capacity to handle economic risks and maintain a balance in international ties.

Constructing a Long-Term AI Environment

Establishing collaborations, funding companies, and encouraging innovation are all necessary to create a viable AI ecosystem. The UAE will need to work closely with international partners, invest in AI firms, and draw talent if it hopes to see its AI strategy through to the end.

Assisting companies and Entrepreneurs: Fostering the expansion of artificial intelligence companies and offering assistance to entrepreneurs will stimulate creativity and generate novel prospects. In order to maintain its leadership in the industry, the UAE will need to continue focusing on developing a thriving AI ecosystem.

Extending AI Education and Research: Funding for AI education and research will promote the advancement of AI technology and help build a skilled labor force.

The UAE's long-term success will be aided by its dedication to growing its research and educational efforts.

Encouraging Worldwide Collaborations:

Establishing and fortifying multinational alliances will augment the United Arab Emirates's worldwide clout and grant entry to a global pool of knowledge. Working together will be crucial to fostering innovation and tackling global AI concerns.

In summary

Abu Dhabi has made great strides toward AI leadership through strategic vision, audacious goals, and noteworthy accomplishments. The United Arab Emirates' AI capabilities have advanced significantly due to its alignment with the United States, which has also enabled access to cutting edge technologies and fostered international collaborations. Future developments in AI in the area and its influence on the international scene will be shaped by the UAE's emphasis on innovation, talent development, and international collaborations.

In order to sustain growth and hold onto its position as a worldwide leader in AI, the UAE will need to address issues including talent development, ethical concerns, and geopolitical factors as it continues to negotiate the complexity of the AI landscape. AI has enormous potential for the UAE in the future, with the possibility for global impact, scientific breakthroughs, and economic revolution. The UAE is in a strong position to continue leading the way in the field of artificial intelligence if it stays true to its strategic objectives and changes with the times.

www.ingramcontent.com/pod-product-compliance
Lightning Source LLC
Chambersburg PA
CBHW071925210526
45479CB00002B/563